HIDE AND SEEK

Evelyn Stone
Illustrated with photographs

HAMPTON-BROWN

Sea animals play hide and seek
all the time. It may seem like a game
to you, but it's not a game in the sea.

Some sea animals need to hide
where they won't get eaten.

And when they want to eat,
they need to go out and find
a meal.

They hide, they peek, and then
they seek! Hide and seek is not
a game in the sea.

Some sea animals feel safe in the seaweed where they are hard to see.

This little sea dragon likes to hide in seaweed. Can you see why?

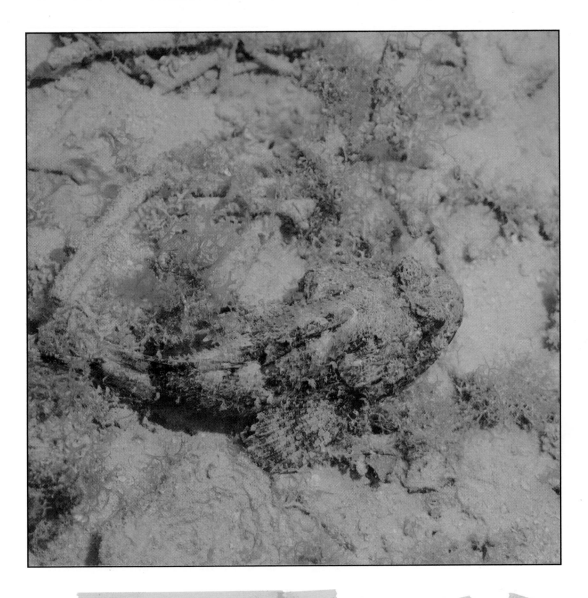

Some sea animals feel safe on the bottom where they are hard to see. This is a stonefish: . It is hiding on the bottom of the sea. Can you see it?

Some sea animals feel safe in the light at the top of the water where they are hard to see.

Needlefish hide in this light.
Can you see them?

Some sea animals feel safe in shells where they are hard to see.
A little crab hides in this shell. Can you see it?

Some sea animals feel safe in caves where they are hard to see. This octopus is hiding in a cave. Can you see it?

When the octopus wants to eat, it hides, it peeks, and then it seeks.

A crab comes by and ZAP!
The octopus finds a meal.
Hide and seek. Hide and
peek. It's not a game in the sea.

Some sea animals feel safe
in the sand where they are hard
to see.

This manta ray hides in the
sand. Can you see it?

Some sea animals feel safe in holes where they are hard to see. This eel hides in a hole. Can you see it?

When the eel wants to eat, it hides, it peeks, and then it seeks. A fish comes by and ZAP! The eel finds a meal.

Hide and seek. Hide and peek. It may be a game to you, but it's not a game in the sea.